Hogarth's Times

HOGARTH'S TIMES

A Harlot's Progress
The Rake's Progress
The Four Stages of Cruelty
Beer Street : Gin Lane
Industry and Idleness
Marriage-à-la-Mode

Edited by Michael Alexander

Miniature Books

THE RODALE PRESS

Published in 1956 by
THE RODALE PRESS
123 New Bond Street, London, W.1
and in the U.S.A. by
RODALE BOOKS INC.
Emmaus, Pennsylvania

Printed in England
at the Pitman Press, Bath

Introduction

The Hogarth serial prints have been alive for two hundred years. Whether bought for a shilling at The Golden Head in Leicester Fields on the day of publication, peered at through fly-blown glass on the darkened staircase, or thumbed in the expensive and massive volumes complete with equally massive commentaries and moralizings that have appeared down the years, they have given to innumerable Englishmen a fascinating study of men and manners, of London and its life. Today there is no edition of the plates available at a low price and it is the object of this book to bring Hogarth back before the public for whom he drew. ·

The commentary to the pictures by that worldly divine the Rev John Trusler has necessarily been sternly edited, but it is hoped that something of his fine flow of Georgian rhetoric still remains. This, together with the notes, which derive from a variety of sources and make no attempt to be exhaustive, may provide an incentive to further speculation and research and perhaps induce idle readers to look into the pictures as well as at them.

MICHAEL ALEXANDER

A Note on the Plates

These reproductions from Hogarth's own engravings (with the exception of Marriage à la Mode, see note) were made mainly from 2nd state impressions which were selected for the additional details they contained. They were made available through the courtesy of the Victoria and Albert Museum.

A Note on the Reverend John Trusler (1735-1820)

Son of the proprietor of the public tea-gardens at Marylebone. Educated Westminster and Cambridge. Translated several Italian comic operas. Took holy orders in 1759. Established an academy for teaching oratory 'mechanically' but gave it up as it did not pay. Studied medicine in Leyden.

Superintended for some time The Literary Society established in 1765 with the object of abolishing publishers. Sent circulars to every parish in England and Ireland proposing to print, in imitation of handwriting, 150 sermons for 1s. to save clergy both study and the trouble of transcribing. Scheme met with considerable success. Established successful publishing enterprise and retired on the profits.

Mrs Hogarth advertised in the London Chronicle of 1766 that she had

'engaged a gentleman to explain each print, and moralize on it in such a manner as to make them as well instructive as entertaining'.

But in his *Biographical Anecdotes* (1785) George Stevens puts the transaction in a different light:

'The Rev John Trusler engaged with some engravers in this design, after Hogarth's death, when they could carry it into execution with impunity. Mrs Hogarth, finding her property would be much affected by it, was glad to accept an offer they made her, of entering into partnership with them; and they were very glad to receive her, knowing her name would give credit to the publication, and that she would certainly supply many anecdotes to explain the plates. Such as are found in the work are probably all hers.'

The resulting work, *Hogarth Moralized*, from which our commentary is extracted, was published in 1768.

A Harlot's Progress

A Harlot's Progress · 'Wm. Hogarth inv^t pinx^t et sculp$^{t'}$ 1732.

[Hogarth's original paintings of this series from which he engraved the plates belonged to W. Beckford (author of Vathek) and were destroyed in the fire of 1755 at Fonthill.]

NOTES ON THE PLATES

I. The procuress is Mother Needham who died as a result of having been 'ungratefully used by the populace in a pillory'.

Col. Francis Charteris. Convicted of rape, Old Bailey 1730, on the evidence of Anne Bond, a servant in his employ.

II. Hogarth took every opportunity of burlesquing the fashion for collecting bogus old masters from the Continent at the expense of the English school. He referred to them as the 'Black Masters' because it was thought that coats of varnish and dirt added to their value. (See etching 'Time Smoking a Picture', of 1761.)

III. This Pastoral Letter was written by Dr Gibson, Bishop of London.

The magistrate is Sir John Gonson who gained the name of the 'harlot-hunting Justice'.

V. The doctor is possibly Misaubin, a quack. (See Marriage à la Mode, note to Plate III.)

VI. The woman on the left is Elizabeth Adams who was executed for robbery in 1737. The clergyman is 'a certain dissolute Chaplain of the Fleet'. The sobbing lady on the right represents a procuress called Bentley.

The sprigs of yew are to guard against infection. The plate on the coffin is inscribed 'M. Hackabout. Died September 2nd 1731. Aged 23'. The Grub Street Journal for August 6th 1730 gives an account of various prostitutes arrested, including one Kate Hackabout of Drury, whose brother was hanged at Tyburn.

I. THE INNOCENT GIRL BECOMES A HARLOT

The first scene of this domestic tragedy is laid at the Bell Inn, in Wood Street, Cheapside; the heroine of the piece, about sixteen years of age, is supposed to be just alighted from the York waggon, accompanied by her father, a poor country curate, on horseback, in search of a better fortune.

These prints were first published in the time of the notorious Colonel Chartres, a man of some fortune, which he appropriated to the worst of purposes, that of accomplishing the ruin of virgin innocence; to effect this horrid end, he kept in his pay a number of men and women, who made it their business to delude the unknowing. This wretch is here exhibited as looking from an ale-house door in company with a flattering pander, who is considering this artless maid already as his prey, while his vile procuress is endeavouring to ensnare her unsuspecting innocence. She is here supposed offering to take her as her servant, and the raw country girl, amused and dazzled with the artful tale, readily embraces the offer, and thus falls a victim to her vile betrayer.

II. THE HARLOT FINDS A PROTECTOR

Entered into the path of infamy, the next scene exhibits our young
heroine the mistress of a rich Jew. Having quitted her innocence with
her modesty of attire, she now keeps up the spirit of the character she
professes, in giving way to extravagance and inconstance. The Jew is
represented as having arrived early in the morning, to breakfast with
his mistress, before the departure of his rival; for notwithstanding these
women are indulged in every thing they can wish, they seem determined to gratify their inclinations, at the expense of their future
welfare; having once bid adieu to virtue, neither honour nor gratitude
can afterwards stop them in their career of vice. His unexpected visit
gives a general alarm, and instantly calls forth the subtile invention
both of her and her maid, in order to devise some means of favouring
her spark's escape; she readily effects that by taking an opportunity of
quarrelling with her keeper, and in a pretended passion, overturns the
table; the clattering noise of which, and the surprise it occasions, added
to the scalding of his leg, so engages his attention, as to give the other
an opportunity of escaping unnoticed.

III. THE HARLOT'S FALL

Observe here the child of misfortune fallen from her high estate. Every valuable she once possessed is now gone and her magnificent apartment now dwindled into a beggarly room in the purlieus of Drury, as is plain from the inscription on the pewter pots. She has now commenced a dishonest career, and is sending out a watch to pawn, which perhaps she had stolen from her last gallant. Proof of the company she keeps is the wig box on the tester of the bed, which we are told formerly belonged to one James Dalton, a notorious street-robber, afterwards hanged. It is not beggary only that is the lot of these unhappy wretches, but disease also lends its baneful influences to heighten their misery, as is intimated by the phials, etc., in the window.

By the piece of butter wrapt up in the title-page of a Pastoral Letter is shown the great degeneracy of the age in matters of religion.

There are many other little objects in this plate, met with in the chamber of the prostitute, that sufficiently explain themselves; we shall therefore only direct the attention to the magistrate entering her room, in order to convey her to the house of correction.

IV. THE HARLOT LODGED IN BRIDEWELL

We here then behold our wretched female lodged in company with pick-pockets, sharpers, and others of her own stamp, of all ranks and ages, reduced to the miserable alternative of beating hemp. In this horrid receptacle various kinds of punishment are inflicted: some are obliged to drag a heavy clog locked to their legs; some are stapled to the ground; while others are hung for an hour by the wrists, or fastened to a post and whipped; but all are made to labour hard, being subject to the correction of a savage task-master, who reaps the profits of their labour.

To show that neither the dread nor endurance of the severest punishment will deter from the perpetration of crimes, a one-eyed female, close to the keeper, is picking a pocket. The torn card may probably be dropped by the well-dressed gamester, whose laced hat is hung up as a companion trophy to the hoop petticoat.

One of the girls appears scarcely in her 'teens. To the disgrace of our police, these unfortunate little wanderers are still suffered to take their nocturnal rambles in the most public streets of the metropolis.

V. THE HARLOT FALLS SICK

Released from confinement, we now view her expiring in all the extremity of penury and wretchedness. The two quacks are quarrelling whose medicine was the best, and over-turn the table, without paying the least attention to the expiring patient. That this inattention to any but ourselves is general among all ranks of people is shewn by the nurse's rifling her mistress's trunk for plunder, ere the breath has well left her body. The only one properly engaged is the child (the innocent fruit of her crimes), busied in turning the meat that is roasting at the fire.

In this pitiable situation, without a friend to close her dying eyes, or soften her sufferings by a tributary tear; forlorn! destitute! and deserted! the heroine of this eventful history expires; her premature death brought on by a licentious life, seven years of which had been devoted to debauchery and dissipation, and attended by consequent infamy, misery, and disease. The whole story affords a valuable lesson to the young and inexperienced, and proves this great, this important truth, that a deviation from virtue is a departure from happiness.

VI. THE HARLOT'S FUNERAL

The company here assembled are of our heroine's profession. The room
presents many things met with at funerals, such as the escutcheon (viz.
the arms of her profession, three spigots and fossets), the giving of
gloves and mourning rings, etc. In the corner sits an old procuress,
howling for the dead, with a bottle of nantz by her side. View the
undertaker, unappalled at the ghastly corpse, fixing his lustful eye upon
the woman whose glove he is pulling on, and she unaffected at the
awful solemnity, artfully robbing him of his handkerchief. Near the
door are two mourners in all the pride of affliction; one of whom is
turning up her eyes, and pouring forth hypocritical ejaculations, which
they do not feel. Even the minister is particularly employed with his
agreeable neighbour, who has in her hand a sprig of rosemary,
formerly distributed on these occasions. The boy winding up his top,
keeps up the spirit of the piece. Thus we see the farce of life carried
on, even to our latest hours; and we continue our follies without inter-
mission to the grave.

The Rake's Progress

The Rake's Progress · 'Invented, printed and engraved by Wm. Hogarth and published according to Act of Parliament June 25 1735.'
[The original paintings are now in the Soane Museum.]

NOTES ON THE PLATES

II. The fencing master is Dubois, a Frenchman who was killed by an Irishman of the same name in a duel fought in Marylebone Fields in 1734. The man with staves is James Figg, the famous prize-fighter who died in 1734. The landscape gardener is Bridgeman. The harpsichord is inscribed 'T. Mohoan fecit'. The player may possibly be Handel. The long roll of paper is inscribed: 'A list of the rich presents Signor Farinelli the Italian condescended to accept of ye English Nobility and Gentry for one Night's performance of the opera of Artaxerxes.' The last of the presents on the list is 'A Gold Snuffbox chac'd with the Story of Orpheus charming Ye Brutes, by T. Rake-Well Esq.'
Farinelli was a popular Italian male soprano (counter-tenor).

III. Rose Tavern next door to Drury Lane Theatre. The dish is borne by Leathercoat the muscular porter at the Rose who was remarkable for his knowledge of the women of the town. For a pot of beer he would lie down in the street and allow a carriage to pass over him.
The pictures are Roman Emperors, which except for Nero are not placed in their proper order. In the frame of Caesar is a portrait of Pontack who kept a celebrated eating tavern in Abchurch Lane.

IV. It is the birthday of Queen Caroline.
White's Chocolate House—Opened 1693 by Francis White at 38 St James Street.
The Farthing Post—a newspaper sold for a farthing (probably without stamps thus defrauding the revenue).
The shirtless street boy was painted from a French shoeblack.

V. Marylebone Church. Pulled down in 1741. The church now in Marylebone High Street was built on its site. The dog on the right represents Hogarth's favourite, Trump.

VI. The gambler borrowing money is supposed to be 'old Manners', brother to the Duke of Rutland, who won the great estate of Leicester Abbey. White's was a noted headquarters of gaming. On the left an elegant nobleman borrows from a money-lender who is writing in a memorandum book, 'Lent to Ld. Cogg 500L.'
The card on the wall bears the royal arms and the inscription, 'R. Justian, Card-maker to his Maj[esty]—royal family'.
In 1733 White's was entirely destroyed by fire.

VII. The Fleet Prison. For debtors. Burned down in the Great Fire of 1666, rebuilt in 1670. Destroyed in the Gordon Riots in 1678, rebuilt 1781. Finally taken down in 1844.

The letter reads: 'S^r. I have read y^r play and find it will not doe.' The peculiar spelling is said to ridicule John Rich, Manager of Convent Garden and producer of the Beggar's Opera. His want of education was notorious.

VIII. Bedlam or Bethlehem for lunatics in Moorfields. At one time the hospital 'derived a revenue of at least £400 a year from the indiscriminate admission of visitors'. In 1770 the authorities forbade visitors on the grounds that they 'tended to disturb the tranquility of the patients'.

I. THE YOUNG HEIR TAKING POSSESSION

Here we see our hero just arrived from Oxford on the death of his miserly father, whose room contains many monuments of his avarice; the useless old coat, the worn-out boot, the spectacle frame without glasses, all deemed worthy of preservation; the memorandum 'May 5, 1721. Put off my bad shilling,' an old shoe soled with the cover of a Bible, the jack and spit—those original instruments of hospitality—locked up for fear of being used, the empty chimney, the emaciated cat, the escutcheons bearing the arms of the covetous, viz. three vices hard screwed with the motto 'Beware'. The principal figure from the unmeaning vacancy of his face, appears to have been favoured by nature for a dupe. To commence the delusive swing of pleasure his first application is to the tailor, here measuring him, while the pettifogging attorney seizes the opportunity of plundering his employee. A poor girl enters, whom our hero has seduced under professions of love and promises of marriage, evident from the ring and the letters in her mother's lap. But not even her tears and pregnant condition could awaken in him a spark of tenderness. He violates every former protestation and attempts to bribe her into silence while the mother loads him with reproaches.

II. SURROUNDED BY ARTISTS AND PROFESSORS

See now our prodigal son at his levee, attended by masters of various professions, here offering their interested services. The foremost figure is a dancing-master; behind him are one, a Frenchman, teacher of the small sword, and an Englishman, master of the quarter-staff; on his left stands an improver of gardens, offering a plan. A professor of music sits at the harpsichord, behind whose chair hangs a list of the presents, one Farinelli received after his first performance at the Opera House. A poem is on the floor, which represents the ladies of Britain crying out, with the greatest earnestness, 'one G—d, one Farinelli.' Beside our hero is one whom we may easily discover to be a bravo; he has brought a letter of recommendation, as one disposed to undertake all sorts of service. It is evident, from his rider bringing in a silver punch-bowl, which one of his horses is supposed to have won, and his saloon being ridiculously ornamented with the portraits of celebrated cocks, that our hero has imbibed a taste for cock-fighting and horse-racing. Besides a poet, the figures in the background represent tailors, peruke-makers, milliners, and such other rapacious persons as generally fill the antechamber of a man of quality.

III. THE TAVERN SCENE

Our licentious prodigal is here revelling at a low tavern. Behold this
deluded son of dissipation, after having 'beat the rounds', overset a
constable of the night, and knocked down a watchman, evident from
his naked sword, the staff and broken lanthorn, and so absolutely
drunk as not to notice that the girl whose hand is in his bosom is
conveying his watch to her accomplice. The company, having been at
high romps, is now seated in order further to indulge their loose
inclinations. A little ragged wench has been called in to bawl out
ballads of obscenity, and two blind street musicians to accompany her.
Two of the company are at high words, one of whom is spouting wine
at her companion's face, the other in return threatening her with a
knife; behind them is another, in excess of anger at being neglected,
wantonly setting a candle to the map of the world.

In front is a woman stripping herself, in order to exhibit some
indecent postures; the large pewter dish being an apparatus of one
of her positions. By such kinds of libidinous entertainment the debau-
chee gives loose to his desires, and indulges himself at the expense
of everything that is decent, rational, and manly.

IV. ARRESTED FOR DEBT AS GOING TO COURT

By such excesses our hero is reduced to debt. See him arrested by a
sheriff's officer as he is going to court in a sedan chair; it being the
Queen's birthday, which happened to be the first of March, the day
sacred to the tutelar saint of Wales. This sufficiently appears by the
significant strut of the Welchman, proud of the enormous leek, which
he carries in his hat. During this unexpected disaster of our fashionable
spendthrift, the young woman he formerly seduced, now a milliner,
very opportunely passes by, pays the debt and sets him at liberty.

In this view of St. James's we have, at the same time, that of White's
Chocolate house, the rendezvous of the first gamesters in London. By
way of contrast, our author has represented an assembly of shoe blacks,
chimney-sweepers, postillions, and others, gaming with the greatest
earnestness; and distinguished it in opposition to that of White's by the
the name of Black's. We are shown also the various ways of gaming
amongst the lower class of people, such as the tricking cups and balls,
the pricking in the belt, the throwing of dice and the playing of cards.
One is supposed to have lost his clothes, and is proposing to play for
his basket and brushes.

V. MARRIES AN OLD MAID

Unable now to discharge his debts our hero has no other means of sheltering from the impending storm than by a union with an old rich widow. Behold him at the altar, with the deformed and wasted sybil who is to recruit his fortune. Observe his amorous leer upon the girl behind which his affected bride imagines to be directed to herself, and which she returns with a squint of satisfaction. They are supposed to have retired to the church of St. Mary-le-Bone; but secret though he thought to keep the wedding, it did not fail to reach the ears of that unfortunate young woman, whom he had formerly seduced, and who is here represented as entering with her child and mother in order to prevent the solemnization. They are, however, opposed by the pew-opener, lest through an interruption of the ceremony she should lose her customary fee.

VI. SCENE IN A GAMING HOUSE

Flushed now with money we view our hero at a gaming-table, at midnight, in company with gamesters, highwaymen and sharpers. Behold him, after a run of ill-luck, upon his knees, in a desperate fit of phrenzy, gnashing his teeth, and imprecating divine vengeance on his head. On his left hand sits a highwayman, by the fireside (which is covered with a grate, to prevent such accidents as may accrue from the rage of the company) vexed to his soul to think he should have lost in a short space of time, that, in the obtaining of which he had hazarded his life; and so absorbed is he in reflection as not to observe the boy who is bawling to him to take his water. Behind him stands one who has met with the same fate, biting his nails in anger. At the small table sits an usurer lending money to one of the gamblers at an exorbitant interest. Further back is another loser striking with his naked sword at the person supposed to have won his money and whose murder he would certainly have accomplished if not prevented by the intervention of another. To add to this scene of horror and confusion, fire is discovered to issue from the wainscot; this indicates that the hope of the gamester is but as smoke, and that his pernicious vice is as destructive as fire itself.

VII. PRISON SCENE

From the gaming-house our hero passes into a prison, a very natural
transition. Having sold his all he at last attempts to write a play, which
is just returned by the Manager of the theatre saying that his piece
would by no means do. His wife bitterly upbraids him for concealing
from her his former connections (with the unhappy girl, who is here
present with the innocent offspring of her amours, fainting at the sight
of his misfortunes). The under-turnkey presses him for his prison
fees, and the boy refuses to leave the beer he ordered without being
first paid for it. One of the papers falling from the lap of the man who
has started up to assist the fainting mother, contains a scheme for paying the national debt; so infatuated do we find him with his great
affaire as not to bestow a few minutes on the decency of his person. In
the back is one who owes his ruin to an indefatigable search after the
philosopher's stone. Hence we are taught by these characters as well
as by the pair of wings, with the help of which some emulator of
Dedalus intended to escape from his confinement, that more owe
their misfortunes to wild and romantic notions, than to any accident
they meet with in life.

VIII. SCENE IN A MADHOUSE

In this last distressing scene our hero is raving in all the dismal horrors
of hopeless insanity, attended by the faithful and kind-hearted female
whom he so basely betrayed. In an inner room a despairing wretch
implores Heaven for mercy; in the next is one drawing lines upon
a wall to find out the longitude; another looks through a paper, by
way of a telescope, while a crazy tailor stares at him with a sort
of wild astonishment. Behind, another, with his book upon his head,
plays on the violin, intimating that too great a love for music has
been the cause of his distraction. On the stairs sits another, crazed
by love (see the picture round his neck, and the words 'charming
Betty Careless' upon the banisters) and wrapt up so close in melancholy pensiveness as not even to observe the dog that is flying at him.
One who imagines himself the Pope, and is saying mass; another
fancies himself a king, and is casting contempt on his imaginary
subjects by an act of the greatest disdain. Two women spectators are
introduced, walking in the gallery, one of whom is supposed, in a
whisper, to bid the other observe the naked man, which she takes an
opportunity of doing by a leer through the sticks of her fan.

The Four Stages of Cruelty

Four Stages of Cruelty · 'Design'd by W. Hogarth. Published according to Act of Parliament. Feb. 1 1751.' Price 1s.

The leading points in these, as well as the two succeeding prints (Beer Street and Gin Lane) were made as obvious as possible in the hope that their tendency might be seen by men of the lowest rank. Neither minute accuracy of design, nor fine engraving were deemed necessary, as the latter would render them too expensive for the persons for whom they were intended to be useful. . . . 'The prints were engraved with the hope of in some degree correcting the barbarous treatment of animals the very sight of which renders the streets of our Metropolis so distressing to every feeling mind. If they have had that effect and checked the progress of cruelty, I am more proud of having been the author, than I should be of having painted Raffaelle's Cartoons.'

Anecdotes of William Hogarth, T. B. Nichols, 1833

NOTES ON THE PLATES

I. Tom Nero carries on his arm the badge of St Giles' Charity School.
The custom of burning out the eyes of birds was chiefly practised on bullfinches in order to make them sing.

II. Thavies Inn, Chancery, Holborn.
The four lawyers have clubbed together to travel from there to Westminster Hall, the longest shilling fare in London.
A law forbade riding in a cart without a person to watch the horses.
John Broughton (1705–1789). Famous prize-fighter. Invented gloves for boxing.

III. The letter reads: 'Dear Tommy, My mistress has been the best of women to me, and my conscience flies in my face as often as I think of wronging her; yet I am resolved to venture body and soul to do as you would have me, so do not fail to meet me, as you said you would; for I shall bring along with me all the things I can lay my hands on. So no more at present, but I remain yours, 'till death. Ann Gill.'

IV. Probably the Barber-Surgeons Company in Monkwell Street.
It has been suggested that the president in the chair resembles the eminent surgeon John Freke, who was a friend of Hogarth's.
The two skeletons are of James Field, the bruiser, and Maclane. Both were hanged.

I. FIRST STAGE OF CRUELTY

Several groups of boys are here seen at their barbarous diversions.
One is tying a bone to a dog's tail. Another is burning out the eyes
of a bird. Behind some boys hang up two cats to make them fight.
From a window, is one throwing out a cat, with a pair of blown-up
bladders designed to prolong her fall. In the centre we see Tom Nero
piercing a dog with an arrow, heedless of the young gentleman of
better education who, with tears in his eyes, pleads on behalf of the
tortured animal, and even offers his tart for its redemption.

II. SECOND STAGE OF CRUELTY

Tom Nero, now a hackney-coachman, is cruelly beating his horse, and so sensible is the afflicted creature of the unkindness that we perceive the big round drop trickling down his cheek. A passer-by is taking the number of his coach. A cattle driver is beating a lamb and a drayman, asleep, runs over a child. A man goads an overladen ass and others are seen baiting a bull. Cockfighting is intimated upon the wall, as is Broughton's Amphitheatre, where men were often engaged to fight with broadswords.

III. CRUELTY IN PERFECTION

Tom Nero's wicked turn of mind has soon led him upon the road.
He has made himself acquainted with a young servant girl, and having
gained her affection, prevails on her to plunder her mistress, and meet
him at midnight. She keeps the fateful assignation, laden with valuables.
To screen himself from detection and also to rid himself of an expected
incumbrance (for the woman is evidently pregnant), he commits the
horrid deed. In the struggle for life, her shrieks alarm the servants of
an adjoining house, who run too late to her assistance.

IV. THE REWARD OF CRUELTY

Tom Nero, condemned to execution, is afterwards sent to Surgeon's Hall for dissection and a lecture read upon his body. Behold, and shudder at the ghastly sight! See his tongue pulled from the root, his eyeballs wrung from their sockets, and his heart torn from his body, which the dog is gnawing beneath the table! Skulls and bones are boiling in a caldron, afterwards to be linked together by wires. Two of these skeletons we observe above pointing to the Physician's or Surgeon's Arms upon the chair; viz. a hand feeling the pulse.

Beer Street · Gin Lane

Beer Street and Gin Lane · 'Design'd by W. Hogarth. Published according to Act of Parliament Feb. 1, 1751.' Price 1s.

The following announcement appeared in the General Advertiser, February 13 1750–51: 'On Friday next will be published Price 1s. each Two large prints design'd and etch'd by Mr Hogarth call'd Beer-Street and Gin-Lane. A number will be printed in better manner for the curious at 1s. 6d. each . . . N.B. As the subjects of these Prints are calculated to reform some reigning vices peculiar to the lower class of people in hopes to render them of more extensive use, the Author has published them in the cheapest manner possible. To be had at the Golden Head in Leicester fields, where may be had all his other works.'

NOTES ON THE PLATES

Beer Street.

On the left are seen a butcher, a drayman and a cooper. On the table before them is the Daily Advertiser and words from the much-admired post-war speech made by George II on Tuesday the 29th of November, 1748. 'Let me earnestly recommend to you the advancement of our commerce, and cultivating the arts of peace, in which you may depend on my hearty concurrence and encouragement.'

The city porter on the right has set down a load of books consigned to Mr Pastem, trunk-maker, in St Paul's Churchyard, as being fit for nothing but waste paper. Their titles read as follows: Lauder on Milton, Modern Tragedies, vol. 12. Hill on Royal Societies, Turnbull on Ancient Painting, and Politics, vol. 9999.

The two fishwomen are loaded with British herrings which were then very plentiful. One carries a ballad written by Hogarth's friend Lockman on the Herring Fishery and sung at Vauxhall Gardens. Lockman, known as 'The Herring Poet', was secretary to the British White Herring Fishery Company. The sign painter is said to represent the Swiss portrait painter, Jean Etienne Liotard who 'could render nothing but what he saw before his eyes'; hence the bottle suspended as a model.

The lady in crinolines in the background is perhaps going to Court in her sedan-chair, since, from the flag on the church (St Martin-in-the-Fields), it is probably the King's birthday.

Gin Lane.

Gin was at this time as popular as is beer today.

The scene is St Giles' Rookery. Cleared away in the nineteenth century. Now New Oxford Street. The church is St George's, Bloomsbury.

The figure on the right is said to represent one whose cry was 'Buy my ballads, and I'll give you a glass of gin for nothing'.

The gin-measure sign over the gin-cellar reads 'Gin Royal'. Over the doorway is written: 'Drunk for a Penny, Dead drunk for two pence, Clean straw for nothing.'

The two young girls on the right, pledging each other in gin, wear the badge of St Giles' Charity School.

The verses are thought to be by Hogarth's friend, Dr Townly.

BEER STREET

Beer, happy product of our isle,
Can sinewy strength impart;
And, wearied with fatigue and toil,
Can cheer each manly heart.
Labour and art, upheld by thee,
Successfully advance;
We quaff the balmy juice with glee,
And water leave to France.
Genius of health, thy grateful taste
Rivals the cup of Jove;
And warms each English, generous breast,
With liberty and love.

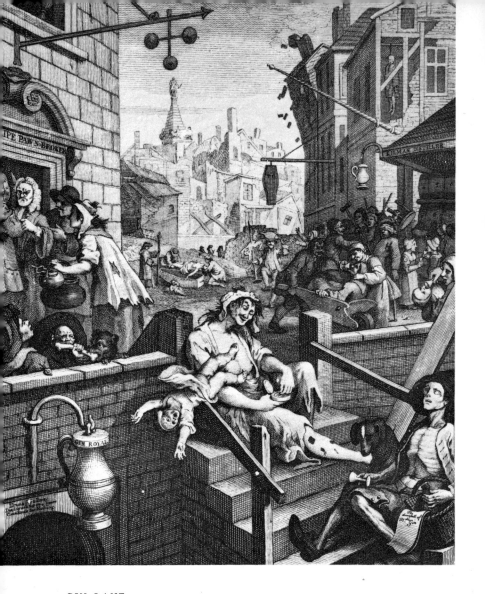

GIN LANE

Gin, cursed fiend! with fury fraught,
Makes human race a prey;
It enters by a deadly draught,
And steals our life away.
Virtue and Truth, driv'n to despair,
Its rage compels to fly,

But cherishes, with hellish care,
Theft, murder, perjury.
Damn'd cup! that on the vitals preys,
That liquid fire contains;
Which madness to the heart conveys,
And rolls it through the veins.

Industry and Idleness

Industry and Idleness · 'Design'd & Engraved by W^m. Hogarth. Publish'd according to Act of Parliament 30 Sep. 1747.'

The following announcement appeared in the General Advertiser for Saturday, October 17 1747: 'This day is published, Price 12s, Design'd and Engrav'd by Mr. Hogarth. Twelve Prints call'd "Industry and Idleness," showing the advantages attending the former and the miserable effects of the latter, in the different Fortunes of Two Apprentices. To be had at the Golden Head in Leicester Fields, and at the Print-shops. There are some printed on better paper for the curious at 14s. each set, to be had only at the Author's in Leicester Fields, Where may be had all his other works.'

NOTES ON THE PLATES

I. Spitalfields, centre of the London silk trade since the coming of the French Protestant refugees after the revocation of the Edict of Nantes, 1685.

V. Cuckold's Point was about three miles below London Bridge.

VI. The inscription on the Monument reads: 'In remembrance—of Burning ye Protestant City by the Treachery of the Papish Faction.
In - year - of our - lo-d 1666.'

VIII. A city hall, possibly the Fishmongers' Company. The portraits include William III—a judge—Sir William Walworth (the Lord Mayor who slew Wat Tyler, leader of the Peasant Revolt, 1381)—Mr Platell (a Frenchman, once curate of Barnet).

IX. The figure to the right in the background wears the uniform of a grenadier.

X. The one-eyed witness is swearing by putting his left hand on the Bible and kisses his thumb instead of the Book. Execution days at Tyburn were public holidays. It was an old custom to release a carrier pigeon.

XI. In the background can be seen the eminences of Hampstead and Highgate.
The ginger-bread seller on the right was known as Tiddy-Doll from his cry.

XII. The scene is the West end of Cheapside at the corner of Paternoster Row.
Frederick, Prince of Wales, and his wife Augusta are on the balcony. The two flags beneath the balcony bear the arms of the Stationers' Company.
So great indeed was the interest taken by the citizens in these civic processions that it was usual to insert a clause in a London lease giving the landlord and his friends the right to stand on the balcony during the time of 'the shows or pastimes, upon the day commonly called the Lord Mayor's Day'.
Decorative borders are common to this series though I–X differ from XI–XII in that fetters, cat-o'-nine-tails and halter compare with golden chain, sword and mace.

I. THE FELLOW 'PRENTICES AT THEIR LOOMS

Here we see the two apprentices at the looms of their master, a silk weaver of Spitalfields. The industrious youth is diligently employed at his work; his book, called the Prentice's Guide, lies open beside him, the employment of the day seems his constant study and the interest of his master his continual regard. The ballads, of the London Prentice, Whittington the Mayor, etc., that hang behind him indicate that he lays out his pence on things that may improve his mind.

On the contrary, his fellow prentice, with worn-out coat and uncombed hair, overpowered with beer, indicated by the half-gallon pot before him, has fallen asleep; and from the shuttle becoming the plaything of the wanton kitten, we learn how he slumbers on, inattentive alike of his own and his master's interest. The ballad of Moll Flanders, on the wall behind him, shows that the bent of his mind is towards that which is bad; and his book of instructions lying torn and defaced upon the ground manifests how regardless he is of anything tending to his future welfare. His master's entering the room with angry countenance, and uplifted cane, shews that his indolence and sloth are visited with present chastisement.

II. THE INDUSTRIOUS 'PRENTICE PERFORMING THE DUTY OF A CHRISTIAN

Here our industrious young man is attending divine service in the same pew as his master's daughter, where he shews every mark of respect and decency, a lively contrast to the man asleep beside him whose conduct shows us how often people are induced to be present on these solemn occasions, merely through fashion, that they may not pass for heathens. The trussed-up figure of the preposterous woman behind him intimates that she is as much swollen with pride as corpulency; that she thinks herself of the greatest consequence, which she endeavours to make known (church being the usual place for such exhibitions) by rivalling her friends in the number of ribbands at her breast, and in the enormous size of her fan, while the figure of the pew-opener on the left denotes the decent behaviour of the devout worshipper: though age and infirmities prevent her from rising, still she pays her adoration to the utmost of her power.

III. THE IDLE 'PRENTICE AT PLAY IN THE CHURCHYARD DURING DIVINE SERVICE

Here we see the Idle 'Prentice, while others are intent on the holy service, gambling on a tombstone with the off-scouring of the people (for none but such would deign to be his companions). Their amusement seems to be the favourite old English game of 'hustle-cap' and our idle and unprincipled youth is endeavouring to cheat by concealing some of the halfpence under the broad brim of his hat. This is perceived by the shoe-black and warmly resented by the fellow with the black patch over his eye (who loudly insists on the hats being fairly removed). The eager anxiety which marks these mean gamblers is equal to that of two peers playing for an estate.

The hand of the boy, employed upon his head, and that of the shoe-black in his bosom, are expressive of filth and vermin.

The blows of the watchful beadle indicate that 'Judgments are prepared for scorners, and stripes for the backs of fools'.

IV. THE INDUSTRIOUS 'PRENTICE A FAVOURITE, AND ENTRUSTED BY HIS MASTER

The Industrious apprentice, by a discreet and steady conduct, attracts the notice of his master, and becomes a favourite; we behold him here in the counting-house (with a distant view of the looms, and of the quilsters winding quills for the shuttles, from whence he was removed) entrusted with the books, receiving and giving orders as appears from the delivery of some stuffs by a city-porter from Blackwell-Hall. By the keys in one hand and the bag in the other we are shewn the confidence that is placed in him. The integrity of his heart is visible in his face, and the familiar position of his master, leaning on his shoulder, is a further proof of his esteem, as is the position of the gloves on the flap of the escritoire. The headpiece to the London Almanack represents Industry taking Time by the forelock.

The strong-beer nose and pimpled face of the porter shew that our author let slip no opportunity of ridiculing the vices and follies of the age, and particularly here in laying before us the strange infatuation of this class of people, who, because a good deal of labour requires some extraordinary refreshment, will even drink to the deprivation of their reason and the destruction of their health.

V. THE IDLE 'PRENTICE TURNED AWAY AND SENT TO SEA

Corrupted by sloth and contaminated by evil company, the idle
apprentice, having tired the patience of his master, is sent to sea. See
him then in the ship's boat, accompanied by his afflicted mother,
making towards the vessel in which he is to embark. The waterman
significantly directs his attention to a figure in a gibbet and the boy
shows him a cat-o'-nine-tails, expressive of the discipline that awaits
him on board ship; these admonitions, however, he notices only by
the application of fingers to his forehead in the form of horns,
jestingly telling them to look at Cuckold's Point, which they have just
passed; he throws his indentures into the water, that proves how little
he is affected by his present condition and how little he regards the
persuasions and tears of a fond mother, whose heart seems ready to
burst with grief at the fate of her darling son, and perhaps her only
stay; for her dress seems to intimate that she is a widow.

VI. THE INDUSTRIOUS 'PRENTICE OUT OF HIS TIME, AND
MARRIED TO HIS MASTER'S DAUGHTER

We now return with pleasure to the industrious youth taken into partnership by his master (evident from the joint names upon the sign), and married to his daughter. The young man appears in his cap and gown from breakfast with his amiable spouse; by the congratulations of the mob we are to suppose that it is the morning after the marriage. Money is being generously given to the necessitous and gold to the master drummer for his comrades. A butcher, standing with his marrow-bone and cleaver, observes the fortunate receiver for the drums; anger is expressed upon the face of his fellow who is elbowing out of the first rank the ruffled French performer on the bass-viol, demanding that precedence the English have always enjoyed. The cripple on the left shows a well-known legless beggar, called Philip-in-the-tub, who was a constant attendant at weddings as an epithalamist. He is supposed to be bawling out the old song of Jesse, or the Happy Pair. In the background stands the Monument.

VII. THE IDLE 'PRENTICE RETURNED FROM SEA AND IN A GARRET WITH A COMMON PROSTITUTE

In this scene we have one of the finest pictures imaginable of the horrors of a guilty conscience. It is clear from the pistols by the bed-side and the trinkets his companion is examining that the Idle 'Prentice has become a highway robber. Though the door is fastened in the strongest manner, though he has attempted to drive away thought by the powerful effects of spirituous liquors, plain from the glass and bottle on the floor, still he is not able to brave out his guilt, or steel his breast against reflection. Behold him roused by the acci-dental circumstance of a cat's coming down the chimney, and the fall-ing of a few bricks, which he believes to be the noise of his pursuers! Observe his starting up in bed, and all the tortures of his mind im-printed in his face; while his wretched bedfellow looks unconcerned at last night's plunder, an ear-ring, two watches, an etwee, and a couple of rings. The phials on the mantelpiece show that sickness and disease are ever attendant on prostitution. The beggarly appearance of the room, the hole by way of window (against which she had hung her old hoop-petticoat in order to keep out the cold) and the rat's running across the floor, are just and sufficient indications that misery and want are the constant companions of a guilty life.

VIII. THE INDUSTRIOUS 'PRENTICE GROWN AND SHERIFF OF LONDON

From industry become opulent, from integrity and punctuality respectable, our young merchant is now Sheriff of London, and dining with the different companies in Guildhall.

A group on the left are admirably characteristic; their whole souls seem absorbed in the pleasures of the table. A divine swallows his soup with the highest goût. Not less gratified is the gentleman palating a glass of wine. The man in a black wig is a positive representative of famine; and the portly and oily citizen, with a napkin tucked in his buttonhole, has evidently burnt his mouth by extreme eagerness. Every person present is so attentive to business that one may fairly conclude that they 'live to eat' rather than 'eat to live'.

At the door is a crowd of people, supposed to have brought a delinquent to justice; one of these has brought a letter addressed to our hero, The Worshipful Francis Goodchild, Esq, Sheriff of London, which the beadle takes with the utmost mark of self-consequence.

IX. THE IDLE 'PRENTICE BETRAYED BY A PROSTITUTE, AND
TAKEN IN A NIGHT CELLAR WITH HIS ACCOMPLICE

In about 1747 when this plate was first published there was a noted
house in Chick Lane, Smithfield, that went by the name of Blood-
Bowl House, so called from the numerous scenes of blood that were
almost daily carried on there; it being a receptacle for prostitutes and
thieves. To this subterraneous abode of iniquity was our hero soon
introduced where he is now represented in company with his accomplice, whom we may recognize as the one-eyed companion of his mis-
spent youth, having just committed a most horrid act of barbarity, that
of killing a passer-by. See them dividing the ill-gotten booty, which
consists of two watches, a snuff-box and some other trinkets. In the
midst of this wicked enjoyment he is betrayed by his strumpet (a proof
of the treachery of such wretches) into the hands of the high constable
and his attendants. The background serves as a representation of night-
cellars in general, those infamous receptacles for the dissolute and
abandoned of both sexes. By the skirmish behind, the woman without
a nose, the scattered cards upon the floor, we are shewn that drunken-
ness and riot, disease, prostitution and ruin are the dreadful attendants
of sloth, and the general forerunners of crimes of the deepest die.

X. THE INDUSTRIOUS 'PRENTICE ALDERMAN OF LONDON; THE IDLE ONE BROUGHT BEFORE HIM, AND IMPEACHED BY HIS ACCOMPLICE

Imagine now this depraved and atrocious youth handcuffed, and dragged from his wicked haunt, to a place of security; and thence brought before the sitting magistrate (his fellow 'prentice, now an alderman) to be dealt with according to the law. He is here seen at the Bar with all the marks of guilt upon his face, suing for mercy and pleading in his cause the former acquaintance that subsisted between them. His one-eyed accomplice betrays him, the proofs are incontestible, the clerk is drawing up instructions for his disposal to Newgate.

Contrast the expression of justice struggling with mercy on the face of the alderman with the corpulent self-swollen constable seeming to say to our unfortunate's mother, 'Make yourself easy, for he must be hanged!' To convince us that bribery will find its way even into courts of judicature, here is a woman in some other cause, feeing the swearing clerk who has stuck his pen behind his ear that his hands might be both at liberty.

XI. THE IDLE 'PRENTICE EXECUTED AT TYBURN

Behold our delinquent on the dreadful morn of his execution; drawn
in a cart (attended by the sheriff's officers on horseback, with his coffin
behind him), through the streets to Tyburn, there to receive the just
reward of his crimes.

This print gives a humorous representation of an execution, or a
Tyburn Fair. See how carelessly one boy watches the motions of a man
selling his cakes, while he is picking his pocket; and another waiting to
receive the booty. In one place we observe an old bawd turning up her
eyes and drinking a glass of gin, the very picture of hypocrisy; and a
man indecently helping up a girl into the same cart; in another, a
soldier sunk up to his knees in a bog, and two boys laughing at him.

In one part is a girl tearing the face of a boy for oversetting her
barrow; in another a woman beating a fellow for throwing down her
child. Here we see a man flinging a dog among the crowd by the tail;
there a woman crying the dying speech of Thomas Idle, printed the
day before his execution. From the gallery a pigeon, bred at the gaol,
is flown, to give an early notice to the keeper of the death of the
criminal. The indifferent executioner is smoking his pipe at the top of
the gallows, further proof that a sad and distressful object loses its
power of affecting by being frequently seen.

Proverbs Chap. III.Ver: 16.
Length of days is in her right hand and
in her left hand Riches and Honour.

XII. THE INDUSTRIOUS 'PRENTICE LORD MAYOR OF LONDON

Nothing remains but to represent out hero's happiness. He is now become Lord Mayor. In front we see the oversetting of a board on which some girls had stood; on the left at the back of the scaffold is a fellow saluting a fair nymph, and another enjoying the joke; near him is a blind man straggled in among the crowd, and joining in the general hollow; before him is a militia-man so completely intoxicated as not to know what he is doing. One, we observe is firing his piece and turning his head the other way. The boy on the right is crying, 'A full and true account of the ghost of Thomas Idle', which is supposed to have appeared to the Mayor.

The most obtrusive figure in his Lordship's coach is Mr Swordbearer, in a cap like a reversed saucepan, which this great officer wears on these grand occasions. The Company of journeymen butchers, with their marrow-bones and cleavers appear to be the most active and are by far the most noisy of any who grace this solemnity. Numberless spectators, upon every house and at every window, dart their desiring eyes on the procession.

Thus we have seen by a series of events the prosperity of one and the downfall of another. Lay the roads but open to the view, and the traveller will take the right course; give but the boy this history to peruse, and his future welfare is almost certain.

Marriage-à-la-Mode

Marriage à la Mode · 'Invented painted and published by Wm. Hogarth According to Act of Parliament April 1 1745.'

Plates engraved 1 and 6 by G. Scotin; 2 and 3 by B. Baron; 4 and 5 by S. Ravenet. The following advertisement appeared in the London Daily Post, April 2 1743: 'Mr Hogarth intends to publish by subscription, Six Prints from Copperplates engrav'd by the best masters in Paris, after his own paintings, representing a variety of Modern Occurrences in High Life, and called Marriage-à-la-Mode. Particular care will be taken, that there may not be the least objection to the Decency or Elegancy of the whole work, and that none of the characters represented shall be personal.'

NOTES ON THE PLATES

I. It has been said that the nobleman represents John Wallop, E. of Portsmouth. The person delivering the mortgage to the Earl is supposed to be one Peter Walter, the 'Peter Pounce' of Fielding's Joseph Andrews.

The pictures on the walls burlesque the French School of painting then in vogue.

II. The apartment is said to be copied from the drawing-room of No. 5 Arlington Street where Horace Walpole lived. Walpole was a great admirer of Hogarth and was one of the first to set a fashion of collecting his prints.

Francis Hayman, Hogarth's friend and copyist, is said to be the model for the husband. The old steward is said to be Edward Swallow, butler to Thomas Herring, the militant Archbishop of York.

The absurd ornaments satirise Kent, the architect who turned his hand with less success to interior decoration. Hogarth's father-in-law particularly detested Kent. Hoyle was the author of the famous treatise on card games.

III. The room is in 96 St Martin's Lane, where lived the notorious quack Dr Misaubin, a Frenchman. Misaubin brought a famous pill into England, by which he made a fortune by questionable means. The unicorn's horn, the pewter basin and the broken comb indicate his former profession as a barber. The woman may be his wife, who prepared his pills.

IV. The book on the couch is 'Sopha', the licentious novel by Crébillon much read at this time.

The singer is said to be Carestini, the Italian male soprano (counter-tenor). The flute-player is Weidemann, who was appointed Assistant Master of Music to George III under Dr Boyce and afterwards Composer of Minuets at the Court of St James.

The excited lady on the sofa is Mrs Fox-Lane (afterwards Lady Bingley) who had a passion for Italian music.

The gentleman in curl papers is said to be Herr Michel, Prussian envoy.

V. The scene may be the Turk's Head Bagnio in Bow Street, Covent Garden, kept by a Mrs Earle.

VI. The old houses on London Bridge were cleared away in 1757 (12 years later). The pictures on the wall satirise the current taste for indifferent Dutch genre pictures.

I. THE MARRIAGE TRANSACTION

A rich tradesman is desirous of a matrimonial alliance with the family of some man of fashion in order to ennoble his family. We may easily imagine that it was not long before he met with the wished-for opportunity, there being many of the English nobility with encumbered estates, always prepared to embrace such an offer. Behold Lord Squander entertaining his proposals; so fond is he of rank, that even his crutches, the mortifying monitors of his infirmities, are ornamented with coronets. He is laid up with the gout; that disorder, in particular, being the usual consequence of irregular living, to which men of quality too often addict themselves. Behind, on a settee, are the bride and bridegroom, in positions of dislike; he taking of snuff and looking in the glass, she playing with her ring, seeming to listen with indifference to the soft things that the young barrister Silvertongue is saying to her. The other counsellor (a serjeant) is examining the plan of my lord's new building, on which he is supposed to have spent the whole of his fortune, not even reserving sufficient to complete it. Two dogs in a corner, coupled together against their inclinations, are good emblems of the ceremony, that is about to take place.

II. THE UNHAPPY PAIR AT HOME

See here the unhappy couple now upon their separate ways. She neglected and incensed, breakfasting at midday, after a night at cards and he, by the female cap in his pocket, returning from the apartments of some woman, fatigued, exhausted and satiated. A sluggard servant comes to set the room to rights while the old faithful steward has taken the opportunity of presenting his accounts. See him then in an attitude of concern dreading the approaching ruin of them both, with but one receipt upon his file.

By the treatise of Hoyle upon the floor we are taught the idle study of people of distinction to whom books in general are disgusting unless they lead to dissipation. There is one other thing which we cannot pass over in silence, and that is an immodest painting in the further part of the room, with a curtain drawn before it; calculated to inflame a wanton imagination, though designedly concealed from public view. A manifest token of the depraved taste of its owner, and a sign of the completion of his vitiated character.

III. A VISIT TO THE DOCTOR

Disease is universally the attendant of debauchery. We are therefore introduced to our hero, at the house of an empiric, where he would have had no occasion to be, had it not been for his lewd course of life. He has brought with him two females, that the doctor might determine to which of the two he might attribute his disorder. His being prejudiced in favour of the girl, occasions a quarrel between him and the woman, which proceeds to great height, even to that of blows. The doctor, a Frenchman, is supposed to have invented two machines, extremely complicated, for the most simple operations; on one of these lies a folio treatise on the nature of these instruments, in French, entitled 'An Explanation of the Two Grand Machines, one for Re-setting the Collar-Bone, the other for Drawing a Cork: invented, by Monsieur De la Pillule: inspected and approved by the Royal Academy at Paris'. In the glass case are three figures, viz. a skeleton of a man that had been executed, intimated by the gallows above, a man in muscles, and a plaster head, on which hangs the doctor's wig.

IV. THE FICKLENESS OF FASHION

Our heroine, by the old peer's death, become a countess, sits at her
toilette. She is just returned from one of the sales of old goods, at
which women of quality are generally duped. Among her purchases
is a figure of Actaeon, to whose horns the boy, with a leer upon his
lady, is archly pointing, as emblematical of the ridiculous appearance
of his master. A fashionable Italian singer commands little attention,
though his jewellery tells us the many presents the ladies have
made him. A country gentleman is fallen fast asleep. Next him sits
one who, by the fan upon his wrist, is more a woman than a man, a
very heretic in love. On the left of him sits another unaccountable,
with his hair in buckle. On a sofa is that young barrister, who seems,
by his picture hanging in this room, to have ingratiated himself in
the favour of the family. He is giving his mistress a ticket for the
masquerade, and pointing to the screen upon which a friar and a nun
in secret converse, intimate the purposes of his heart towards her. A
number of cards lie scattered on the floor, the 'Lady Squander's
company is desired at Lady Heatham's drum-major, next Sunday'
'Lady Squander's company is desired at Miss Hairbrain's rout.'
'Count Rasset begs to know how Lade Squander sleapt last nite.'

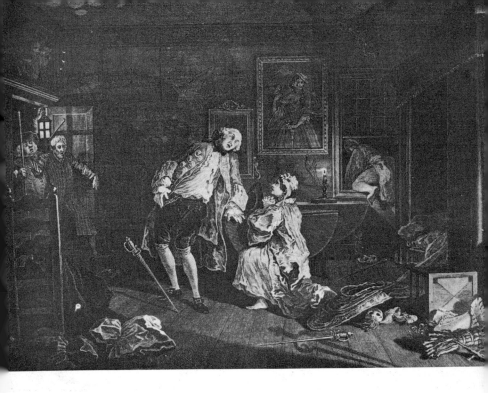

V. THE FATAL CONSEQUENCES

The fatal consequence of going to the masquerade is here shewn to perfection. The ticket was accepted to favour an assignation; the assignation took place, and the catastrophe is dire. Happy was our heroine to find an opportunity of enjoying the company of her spark; happy was the barrister to take an advantage of the supposed weakness of her husband; but behold the end of such illicit and unwarrantable proceedings!—They are supposed to have retired from the ball to some bagnio, in order to gratify their illicit amours. Determined to see the extent of her misconduct, the husband secretly follows; rashly gives them an opportunity of undressing, that he might have the satisfaction of discovering them in bed. A thrust or two passes between them, and the husband is wounded mortally. The noise brings up the watch and a servant of the house, who seem thunderstruck at the ghastly spectacle: alarmed at this accident, the young counsellor secures himself, by escaping from the window in his shirt; and his mistress, struck by remorse and horror, falls on her knees to her dying husband, and, wringing her hands, with tears in her eyes, confesses her guilt, imploring his forgiveness.

VI. THE SAD CONCLUSION

The young barrister is presently taken by the watch, and the next day committed to prison. Madam is conducted to her house, and left to repent her past folly and wickedness. On the report of this melancholy story, the tradesmen of her Lord become urgent and clamorous in their demands. She, therefore, throws her affairs into her father's hands and returns to his house, supposed to be somewhere near London-bridge, for we have a view of it from the window in its original state, when covered with houses. Left to the dreaded leisure of her thoughts, she foolishly thinks she has no other refuge from the terrors of her mind than to destroy herself. In this disordered state she artfully sends a servant for a dose of laudanum, swallows it, and puts an end to her now miserable existence. Behold her then, in the last moments of her life, seized with death, as she and her father were sitting down to dinner. A physician and apothecary are immediately sent for, in vain, it being now too late; the latter severely reprimanding the servant for fetching the deadly potion. An old family servant, in tears, brings the poor little infant, the diseased and rickety offspring of debauched parents, to take its last farewell of its expiring mother.

A NOTE ON WILLIAM HOGARTH (1697–1764)

Born in the City of London. Son of a literary schoolmaster. Apprenticed to the well-known silversmith Ellis Gamble and worked at engraving arms, cyphers, etc., on plate. On the expiration of his apprenticeship entered an art school in St Martin's Lane established by Sir James Thornhill, noted painter of Italianate baroque ceilings at so much per square foot (Greenwich, Hampton Court, etc.). Engraving shop bills, decorating and illustrating books (Hudibras), painting portraits and small conversation pieces afforded him a living for some time. In 1730 clandestinely married Jane Thornhill, only daughter of Sir James, who was reconciled to this marriage by the success of the first great series of moral paintings 'A Harlot's Progress'. Hogarth followed this up with the several series for which he is famous and many single pieces. Appointed in 1757 Serjeant-Painter to George III. Died at Leicester Fields on 25th October 1764. Buried at Chiswick beneath 'a plain but neat mausoleum' bearing the following epitaph by his friend Garrick:

> *Farewell, great painter of mankind,*
> *Who reach'd the noblest point of art*
> *Whose pictured morals charm the mind,*
> *And through the eye correct the heart.*
>
> *If Genius fire thee, reader stay;*
> *If Nature touch thee, drop a tear;*
> *If neither move thee, turn away,*
> *For Hogarth's honour'd dust lies here.*

Hogarth is here shewn with his favourite dog 'Trump'.